T0413386

Queens and Kings

Teaching Tips

Yellow Level 3

This book focuses on the phoneme **/oo/**.

Before Reading

- Discuss the title. Ask readers what they think the book will be about.
- Sound out the words on page 3 together.

Read the Book

- Ask readers to use a finger to follow along with each word as it is read.
- Encourage readers to break down unfamiliar words into units of sound. Then, ask them to string the sounds together to create the words.
- Urge readers to point out when the focused phonics phoneme appears in the text.

After Reading

- Encourage children to reread the book independently or with a friend.
- Guide readers through the phonics exercises at the end of the book.

© 2024 Booklife Publishing
This edition is published by arrangement with Booklife Publishing.

North American adaptations © 2024 Jump!
5357 Penn Avenue South
Minneapolis, MN 55419
www.jumplibrary.com

Decodables by Jump! are published by Jump! Library.
All rights reserved. No part of this book may be reproduced in any form without written permission from the publisher.

Library of Congress Cataloging-in-Publication Data is available at www.loc.gov or upon request from the publisher.

ISBN: 979-8-88524-724-5 (hardcover)
ISBN: 979-8-88524-725-2 (paperback)
ISBN: 979-8-88524-726-9 (ebook)

Photo Credits

Images are courtesy of Shutterstock.com. With thanks to Getty Images, Thinkstock Photo and iStockphoto. Cover - Miras-Wonderland, Alona Syplyak, oksana2010. 4 – Dragon Images. 5 – STUDIO GRAND WEB. 6 – KK Tan. 7 – Guryanov Andrey. 8 – Mark Nazh. 9 – wavebreakmedia. 10 – WilleeCole Photography. 11 – MirasWonderland. 14–15 – Shutterstock.

Can you find these words in the book?

cook

food

good

look

Look! It is the king of the room.

It is the queen of the room too!

This queen has a cool hat. Can you see?

This king needs a cool hat too!

A king and a queen need food.

The cook did a good job! Yum!

Can dogs be good kings and queens?

No! But you can be!

Can you say this sound and draw it with your finger?

Trace the letters /oo/ to complete each word. Say the words out loud.

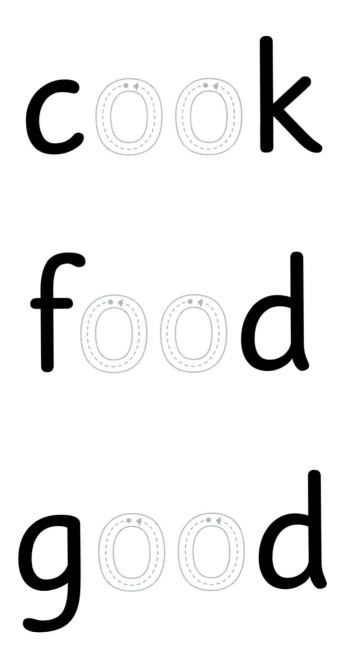

cook

food

good

What other words can you spell with /oo/?

m___n   f___t

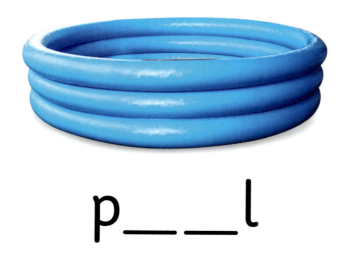

p___l

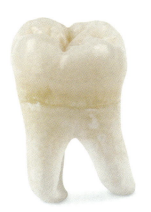

t___ls   t___th

sm___thie

Practice reading the book again:

Look! It is the king of the room.

It is the queen of the room too!

This queen has a cool hat. Can you see?

This king needs a cool hat too!

A king and a queen need food.

The cook did a good job! Yum!

Can dogs be good kings and queens?

No! But you can be!